LAKE DISTRICT
FROM ABOVE

SIMON KIRWAN

Text: JEROME MONAHAN

MYRIAD
LONDON

SOUTHERN LAKE DISTRICT

The Southern Lake District is an area of fell, woodland and coastal expanse. The region is dominated in the north by Grisedale Forest and defined in the south by the river Kent where it emerges into Morecambe Bay. It stretches up as far as the southern shore of Windermere. It is an area rich in tourist opportunities boasting everything from fine walking to some of the best windsurfing in the UK in and around the islands south of Barrow-in-Furness. It is a far less rugged landscape than the rest of the Lakes and has a rich assortment of prosperous and unspoilt market towns to entice the visitor. These include Broughton-in-Furness, at one time a major trading centre, and unspoilt villages such as Arnside and Newby Bridge.

PIEL ISLAND *above*

Piel Island enjoys a rich history. Its first recorded name was Fotheray, derived from the Scandinavian terms for "fodder". In 1127 Piel was given to a local order of Savignac monks, who later merged with the Cistercian order. They developed Piel as a licensed port. On June 4 1487 Lambert Simnel landed at Piel claiming to be the Earl of Warwick (one of the Princes in the Tower) and rightful heir to the throne. He marched his mercenary army south towards Piel but was defeated at Stoke. Instead of being executed, Simnel was allowed to live out his days in King Henry VII's kitchens. The landlord of the Ship Inn on Piel is to this day nicknamed the King of Piel in commemoration of the rebellion.

BARROW-IN-FURNESS *right*

Barrow-in-Furness is sited on the Furness Peninsula which protrudes into Morecambe Bay. It was once a world centre of steelmaking with significant shipyards but those industries are now in decline. Barrow is one of England's few planned towns and it retains its wide, tree-lined streets to this day. There are many fine churches and public buildings including the town hall, a legacy of James Ramsden, the town's first mayor who conceived the idea of Barrow as a shipbuilding centre.

ARNSIDE *left*

The village of Arnside appears to emerge from the thickly-wooded slopes of the Knott – a limestone headland looking over Morecambe Bay. The word "knott" means a rounded hill – one of many local terms thought to be derived from Viking settlers. It was once a busy port trading in slate, gunpowder, coal and pig-iron. The silting up of the Kent estuary, a process exacerbated by the building of the 50-arch railway viaduct across the sands in 1857, finally put paid to the town's marine significance. Today, Arnside is a bustling seaside resort and retirement destination.

BROUGHTON TOWER *below*

Broughton Tower was originally a pele tower, evidence of the Lakes' violent past. It was built in 1322 to defend the Broughton family from cross border raids. The family's fate was sealed, however, when they backed the wrong side in Lambert Simnel's abortive attempt to challenge the Tudor king Henry VII in 1487. It then became the possession of the Stanleys – Earls of Derby until they too backed the losing Royalist cause in the English Civil War (1642-8). Since then the building has been subject to continual extension and alteration. The tower has also been used for many different purposes – from stronghold to family home and then a school. It is now divided into private apartments.

HOAD MONUMENT *right*

Ulverston's outstanding site – a landmark from which there are spectacular views of the Pennines and Morecambe Bay on clear days. It was built in 1850 in honour of the explorer and founder-member of the Royal Geographical Society, Sir John Barrow. The pepperpot-like structure is, in fact, a replica of the Eddystone Lighthouse found south-west of Plymouth. Captain Cook was one of Barrow's great admirers, having used many of his maps on his voyages. Barrow was also the definitive chronicler of the shipboard rebellion in 1789 that became famous as *The Mutiny on the Bounty*.

BIRKER FELL *above*

The remote Birker Fell with Devoke Tarn at its centre is a magnet for ramblers. A popular walk is to circumnavigate the tarn taking in the surrounding summits of Water Crag, Rough Crag, Seat How and White Pike. From here there are superb views north-east towards the high peaks of the western fells including Scafell and west towards the Ravenglass Estuary and the Irish Sea.

NEWBY BRIDGE *right*

This elegant town takes its name from the five-arched stone bridge that spans the river Leven at the southernmost end of Windermere. The photograph is of the bridge and village as it appears looking west. The substantial building in the foreground is the Newby Bridge Hotel, formerly Newby Bridge Mansion. Built in 1793 for the Machel family, it was one of the first great houses on the banks of Windermere.

FELL FOOT *above*

Hundreds of feet above High Parrock Wood, this view is taken looking due east towards Fell Foot Park and Gardens at the southern end of Windermere. Fell Foot was a typical late Victorian garden of rhododendrons, oaks and pines. The great house that once stood at the centre of these atmospheric grounds has long since been demolished, and after many years of neglect the National Trust is undertaking a programme to restore the garden and woods to their former glory. This attractive 18-acre site with picnic areas and boat-hire is open to the public.

CONISTON *below*

The view is taken high above Coniston Water looking back due west at the village of Coniston with Yowdale Beck in the middle distance. Coniston Water is famous as the site of Donald Campbell's death in 1967 during his failed attempt in *Bluebird* to break the world water speed record. Coniston has strong literary associations. The critic and social reformer John Ruskin lived at Brantwood on the shores of the lake and there is a John Ruskin Museum in the town. The children's writer Arthur Ransome used settings around Coniston in his best-selling novel *Swallows and Amazons*.

CONISTON OLD MAN *above*

The Old Man of Coniston is seen here in the foreground; in the distance the shimmering expanse of water is Coniston, from which this peak derives part of its name. The "Old Man" reaches the formidable height of 2635ft (801m). Nearby is the peak known as Wetherlam and between the two lies Levers Water.

LEVERS WATER *right*

One of the most popular of the routes up to Coniston Old Man travels past Levers Water, along Levers Water Beck, through the wonderfully named Boulder Valley and past the Pudding Stone. This vast rock never fails to entice walkers to make the effort to reach its mini-summit despite still having a fairly long haul to the top of Coniston Old Man before them. From the summit there is a clear view of much of the southern Lake District and, in the right conditions, Morecambe Bay, Blackpool Tower and the Isle of Man can be seen.

WESTERN LAKE DISTRICT

The Western region of the Lakes has a coastline which includes the Solway Firth and the Duddon Estuary – a mix of sandy beaches and imposing sea cliffs, estuaries and sheltered coves. Its narrow coastal plain is home to many picturesque villages and hamlets. Further inland are the spectacular valleys of Duddon, Wasdale and Eskdale. Eskdale and the river Esk that runs through it (below) have been described as a "hidden gem". The river rises in the fells at Esk Hause, passes through the Great Moss and enters the valley via a series of waterfalls. On its more lowland course, the Esk waters some of the most stunning oak woodland in Cumbria. Within the valley are numerous delightful villages including Boot, Eskdale Green and Ravenglass.

ST BEES HEAD *above*

St Bees Head is on the western edge of the Lake District. It is a site of beauty for walkers — its four-mile clifftop path is the start of the 190-mile (305km) coast-to-coast walk. This is a dangerous area for shipping and the lighthouse, which dates from 1886-7, is the latest in a series of warning beacons; the rusting hulks of long-forgotten ships can be seen on the shingle at the foot of the 300-foot cliffs. These are a haven for many species of seabird including kittiwakes, herring gulls, razorbills, puffins, ravens, stonechats and red-legged guillemots. Today the site is a bird sanctuary. Legend has it that St Bega — the daughter of an Irish king — was miraculously brought here by an angel. She went on to found a nunnery. The only surviving sign of the local religious order is the red sandstone porch of the parish church surmounted by a lovely carving of St George and the dragon.

WHITEHAVEN *right*

Originally a harbour for the monks at nearby St Bees, Whitehaven really took off in the 17th century thanks to its location near substantial local coal and iron ore reserves. In the 1750s it was England's third most important port but its shallow waters ultimately meant it could not compete with Liverpool. The decline froze the town, preserving its Georgian houses, and today there are over 250 listed buildings. The white round building to the right of the harbour is The Beacon — now a museum celebrating the town's maritime past.

SCAFELL *above* AND SCAFELL PIKE *below*

One of the first prominent non-Lakelanders to climb Scafell was the poet Coleridge. He took with him an ink horn and paper and, having reached the summit, set about recording his feelings to Sarah Hutchinson in a letter dated August 5 1802. He made a helter-skelter descent, ignoring straightforward ways, preferring to take a precipitate direct route down claiming that he was too indolent to bother with looking for other paths. He wrote: *"I ascended Sca'Fell by the side of a torrent, and climbed & rested, rested & climbed, till I gained the very summit of Sca'Fell — believed by the Shepherds here to be higher than even Helvellyn or Skiddaw… O my God! What enormous Mountains these are close by me…"*

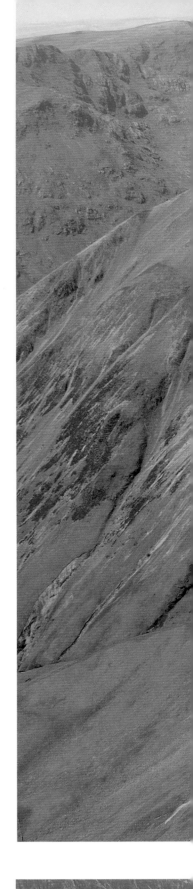

WASDALE *above*

This is one of the most desolate and wild of the Lake District valleys. It is famous for Scafell Pike, England's highest mountain at 3210ft (978m), Wast Water, the region's deepest lake and St Olaf's, one of the smallest churches in England. The valley is fringed with spectacular scree slopes – particularly at Wast Water where they plunge over 2000ft (610m). St Olaf's church is at Wasdale Head and its roof beams are reputed to have once served as the timbers of a Viking longboat. Some of St Olaf's gravestones commemorate climbers who died in the surrounding fells. Every October the Wasdale Show takes place and includes traditional sports, such as hound-trailing.

GREAT GABLE *above*

Great Gable is a beautifully proportioned mountain – so much so that it is used as the centrepiece motif for the Lake District National Park logo. On its slopes can be seen the remains of past industrial times including slateworks and the line of a former tramway. One track named Moses Trod is thought to have been a favourite route for smugglers and their contraband liquor. On clear days climbers and walkers are rewarded with splendid views of Wasdale and the sights at the summit are even more special – the panorama includes every peak in Lakeland.

PILLAR *left*

Pillar Rock is a 500ft (152m) outcrop halfway up to the summit of the Pillar mountain – which at 2926ft (892m) is the eleventh highest summit in the Lakes. The Rock has long been beloved of mountaineers, offering a variety of routes of varying difficulty. It was here in 1913 that the young George Mallory gained early experience ahead of his several attempts on Everest during the inter-war years. One of the climbs is still known as the Mallory route. The mountain itself is considered one of the easier of the big Lakeland peaks to climb – the effort rewarded with awesome views, particularly the 2000ft drop into the Ennerdale Valley.

HIGH CRAG *above*

The High Stile range of peaks
photographed from just below low
cloud casts a brooding presence over
Buttermere and the small settlement of
the same name. The range is made up
of High Crag, High Stile, HayStacks and
Red Pike and is one of the most
popular of the harder walking routes in
the Lakes. To begin with the route is
through woods and waterfalls but this
quickly gives way to open treeless
countryside as you near the summit.

BUTTERMERE *right*

Many claim that Buttermere is one
of the Lake District's most beautiful
locations. Without the unique geology
of the valley of the river Cocker, it
would probably have remained a single
expanse of water, but progressive silting
has resulted in the emergence of three
smaller lakes – Buttermere, Crummock
Water and Loweswater. Buttermere is
about a mile long and approximately
1500ft across and is encompassed by
mountains. It is home to a number of
extremely rare species of fish such as
the Arctic charr. The photograph shows
the view from above Scale Beck looking
south-east towards Buttermere village
and the fertile pasture which separates
Crummock Water from Buttermere.

CRUMMOCK WATER *above*

This sublime stretch of water is situated between Loweswater and Buttermere. The view above Melbreak looks east towards Grasmoor and Whiteless Pike across Crummock Water. Beneath this vantage point is Scale Force. With a single drop of 170ft (52m) it is the Lake District's highest waterfall and one of many mountain rivers that feed the lake. Crummock Water is owned by the National Trust who apply a rigid ban on watersports although those that carry their boats to the lake by hand are allowed to sail or row there. In such a place it is not hard to imagine why the painter John Constable felt the Lake District contained "the finest scenery that ever was".

GRASMOOR *below*

At 2795ft (852m) Grasmoor is an imposing presence on the western side of Crummock Water. It is the highest peak in the group of hills between the villages of Lorton, Braithwaite and Buttermere, the highest of the north-western lake fells. Grasmoor is a favourite challenge for hardier visitors to the Lakes who are rewarded on reaching the summit by a series of ridge-walk circuits taking in wonderful views in all directions. The simplest way up the mountain starts at Braithwaite and proceeds past the former mining areas at Coledale up onto Coledale Hause. The word "gras" has nothing to do with "grass" but derives from *grice* meaning "wild boar".

FLEETWITH PIKE *left*

Stand at the head of Buttermere and look south to where the road snakes its way up the Honister Pass and Fleetwith Pike is an unmistakeable imposing presence. Reaching 2126ft (648m), it is the mass of rock on its flank – the Honister Crags – that make it so memorable.

HAYSTACKS *below*

A favourite spot for Alfred Wainwright, Haystacks offers some fine views of Buttermere, Crummock Water and Ennerdale Water. To the south are the towering crags of the Pillar range whilst to the north is the somewhat less imposing Newlands range. Right beside it are Great Gable and High Stile.

NEWLANDS VALLEY *right*

Close to Keswick, this beautiful valley has not been touched by the commercialism of many other Lakeland valleys. Its farms do a brisk trade in bed and breakfast offering an alternative experience to its more hectic neighbours.

Central Lake District

The heart of the Lake District is a place of wide contrasts with wild mountains, quiet valleys and picturesque villages as well as the lively towns of Windermere, Bowness, Ambleside and Lakeside which prove such a draw for visitors. This area has always been a souce of wonder and inspiration to poets and artists. It was here that Beatrix Potter made her permanent homes at Hill Top and Castle Farm, close to Hawkshead. Earlier, in the 19th century, it was the place where many of the Romantic poets and writers of the day gathered – drawn to the area by its beauty and the presence of William Wordsworth and his family at his homes in Grasmere and at Rydal Mount.

AMBLESIDE *right*

The market town of Ambleside is situated at the northern end of Windermere. It has a long history encompassing Roman and Viking settlement. From the middle ages, its fortunes were wedded to wool-making enhanced, as industrial processes advanced, by the might of nearby Stock Ghyll Force – a 60ft (18m) high waterfall capable of driving a number of watermills. By the late 18th century wool manufacture was in decline but the 1800s saw the start of a tourist industry that again brought prosperity and continues undiminished to the present day. The town's attractions include the Armitt Museum, with its special focus on Beatrix Potter and her animal stories, and the Church of St Mary the Virgin which has a chapel dedicated to William Wordsworth. This church is one of the few that still carries out an annual rushbearing ceremony. This vista north from above Windermere over Ambleside shows the land beyond climbing to Scandale Fell – the source of Scandale Beck that skirts the upper reaches of the town.

BOWNESS-ON-WINDERMERE *left*

This thriving, bustling town straggles for about 12 miles along the western shore of the lake. The view east from the town over the lake is delightful. It includes Belle Isle and the heavily wooded Claife Heights rising to Latterbarrow at 803ft (245m). Bowness owes its greatest period of expansion to the arrival of the railway line from Oxenholme and Kendal in 1847. The town's Victorian roots are unmistakeable thanks to the many late 19th-century residences overlooking the lake built by wealthy Lancashire businessmen. They are now mostly hotels. The old Bowness is preserved to the rear of St Martin's church where there is a labyrinth of narrow streets collectively known as Lowside. When William Wordsworth in *The Prelude* describes bounding *"the hill shouting amain/ A lusty summons to the further shore/For the old Ferryman"* – he is referring to the Bowness ferry that frequently carried him across Windermere.

LOUGHRIGG FELL *right*

Hovering over Loughrigg Fell, the photograph captures the vista to the north looking across the fell towards Grasmere with the pass between The Great Tongue and Grasmere Common plainly visible. Loughrigg Fell is a prominent 1099ft (335m) hill standing at the end of a long ridge dropping down from High Raise. Loughrigg Fell is one of the most popular hills in the Lakes, with over 100 paths to the top. One of the walkers' most popular routes leads to Loughrigg Terrace from where there are magnificent views of Grasmere, Helm Crag and the Fairfield group of mountains. Another attraction on Loughrigg Terrace are some quite remarkable caves formed after centuries of industrial quarrying in the area. They can penetrate to a great depth and are often waterlogged.

LAKESIDE *below*

The view over Lakeside looking south-west reveals the vast Finsthwaite plantation – the tracks of the Lakeside and Haversthwaite Railway clearly visible snaking along the valley beside the Haversthwaite river. Lakeside is a key tourist centre – a hub for sailing enthusiasts and day visitors drawn to the Aquarium of the Lakes with its displays providing insights into the area's unique underwater eco-systems. The steam railway is also a major attraction, giving passengers a chance to experience the golden age of rail travel over its three and a half mile track to Haversthwaite.

THE LANGDALE
PIKES *above & right*

At the southern end of the region, the Langdale Pikes are a group of rocky-topped mountains. They include Harrison Stickle and Pavey Ark (pictured right) with Stickle Tarn sheltering below. Pike of Stickle (pictured above) also known as Pike O' Stickle, reaches a height of 2326ft (709m). It rises steeply from Langdale and culminates in a pyramidal summit from which there are awesome views of the head of the valley, the fells of Bow Fell and Crinkle Crags. Pike of Stickle is famous as the site of a neolithic stone axe factory, discovered on the scree slope on the southern slope of the fell. This was one of the most important pre-historic factories of its kind in Europe. Early man was attracted to this spot by the vein of greenstone, a highly durable igneous rock, which surfaces here.

GRASMERE *above*

Described by Wordsworth as "the loveliest spot that man has found" the lake of Grasmere is a short stroll from the village of the same name. It is in the heart of the Lake District, centrally placed between Ambleside, Keswick and Coniston. Grasmere is probably the most visited village in the Lake District, because of its associations with the Wordsworths – William, his wife Mary and sister Dorothy – who made Dove Cottage their home from 1799 until 1808. Another focal point is the Church of St Oswald where William and his family are buried. Every August the famous Grasmere Sports are held with displays of wrestling, fell-racing and hound-trailing. The village is also the home of the famous gingerbread shop, located in the old schoolhouse close to the church. With the consistency of a spicy shortbread rather than a cake, the gingerbread is made to an original recipe devised by local woman Sarah Nelson in the early 19th century.

DERWENT WATER *right*

Fed by the river Derwent, Derwent Water lies to the south of Keswick. It contains several islands – three of which are to be seen in the photograph. These are Derwent Isle, Lords Island and tiny Rampsholme Island just in view. The steep drop of Lady's Rake Crag is clearly visible in the distance. Friars Crag is the promontory jutting into the lake just beyond Derwent Isle. Friars Crag achieved its name because it was believed to be the embarkation point for monks making a pilgrimage to St Herbert's Island, located in the centre of Derwent Water. It is thanks to Canon Rawnsley, vicar of nearby Crosthwaite Church on the edge of Keswick, that much of this land has been so remarkably preserved. He was a founder of the National Trust. On his death in 1920 Friars Crag was one of several sites given to the Trust as his memorial.

EASEDALE TARN *left*

Two miles from Grasmere, Easedale Tarn lies in a natural amphitheatre. The valley is littered with boulders rounded by the force of ice scraping over them. Sour Milk Gill, so called because of its white churning water, exits from the tarn. According to the poet Thomas de Quincey, Easedale Tarn was "a chapel within a cathedral" and "the most gloomily sublime" of all the tarns he knew.

BOWFELL *below*

This pyramid-shaped mountain is located in the southern fells area. The view north-west over Bowfell is one of the most spectacular in the Lakes looking out onto Great End and the Great Gable heights. It lies to the east of Scafell. Among its attractions are the Great Slab and the drop down over the crag at Bowfell Links. Bowfell is an impressive mountain, flanked to the south by Crinkle Crags and to the north by the Langdale Pikes. Most people climb this mountain up a path called The Band. The panoramic views from the summit are breathtaking with the Pennines to the east and, on clear days, the sight of the Isle of Man to the west.

EASTERN LAKE DISTRICT

The eastern part of the Lake District is dominated by a great north to south ridge – the Helvellyn Range. This runs from Clough Head with its grassy slopes to Seat Sandal. Helvellyn has been described as "a wall of ten miles of 2500 feet plus summits with grassy western slopes, but impressive rocky corries and crags on the eastern side". One of the most famous of the peaks is collectively known as the Fairfield group and this is found at the south of the range. It too follows the same pattern of slope and crag with towering rock faces and hidden valleys spilling into the Patterdale valley. The Fairfield group culminates in the harsh landscape overlooking the Kirkstone Pass – the highest road in the Lakes and a bleak spot famous for its apparitions. The far eastern fells lie on the other side of Patterdale. High Street is one of its most famous landmarks and at 2717ft (828m) is the highest point on the ridge. It boasts spectacular crags dropping to the hidden valleys of Mardale and Haweswater. To the south are the fells overlooking Kentmere.

HAWESWATER *above* AND HAYESWATER *right*

The serpentine Haweswater Reservoir (above) fills the valley between Bampton Common in the west and Swindale Common to the east. When the valley was flooded in 1935 to create a water supply for Manchester, the main casualties were the picturesque villages of Mardale Green and Measand, both of which were demolished. Among the most significant losses was the ancient Dun Bull Hotel at Mardale Green. The village church was dismantled and the stone used to construct the dam, and all the bodies in the churchyard were exhumed and re-buried at Shap. During periods of drought the remains of the village's buildings are revealed and invariably hit the headlines.

Hayeswater Reservoir (right) lies a few miles to the west, near Hartsop. The photograph shows the distinctive curved ridge of High Street, named after the Roman road that ran over its summit, linking the forts of Brocavum near Penrith and Galava at Ambleside.

KENDAL AND KENDAL CASTLE

Kendal's limestone buildings have earned it the nickname "The Auld Grey one" and its location has consolidated it as the "Gateway to the Lakes". Kendal is often overlooked by visitors eager to press on to the Lake District proper, but to do so is to miss out on the charms of this underestimated town. Among its treasures is Holy Trinity Church – Cumbria's largest parish church. The local museum is also a must-see with a permanent exhibition dedicated to Alfred Wainwright whose sketches and descriptions of his favourite walks have popularised visiting and walking in Cumbria and beyond. The photograph shows the view north across the town with the river Kent in view.

Kendal Castle commands high ground to the west of the town. The surviving remains are of a 12th-century structure and they include two towers and connecting stone ramparts. Its presence is a reminder of Kendal's violent past – frequently invaded by the Scots. Richard II granted the castle to the Parr family, but it is thought unlikely that Katherine Parr, Kendal's most famous daughter, was actually born there. Today, the landscaped slopes beneath the ruins are a favourite spot for walking and picnics.

RED TARN *left*

This upland tarn, high above Patterdale Common, is so-named because it resembles the colour of mercury when observed from the east. It is often cited as the perfect example of a corrie – the birthplace of a glacier. In a former Ice Age a "niche glacier" would form once an accumulation of snow reached a certain size and underlying pressure. The increased erosion both above and below ground ("nivation") would eventually create amphitheatre-type hollows with a characteristic rock "lip". It is this shape that means a corrie accumulates water in times when the glaciers retreat. Today Red Tarn is home to the schelly – one of the Lakes' three protected species of freshwater fish.

THIRLMERE *below*

The view north along Thirlmere shows the wooded slopes to the west that form the foothills of High Seat in the distance. To the east Great How, also heavily wooded with spruce and larch, emerges from the valley floor. The original Thirlmere was a smaller lake than it is today, but the need for water in Manchester necessitated the building of a dam at the valley's north end between 1890 and 1894 and flooding of the valley bottom. Thirlmere, once an isolated place, has now been opened up by the presence of a minor road, plainly in view in the photograph on the western side. An effort is also being made to transform the woodland to create a more mixed habitat.

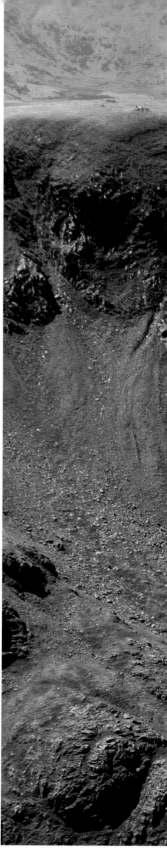

HELVELLYN *left*

At 3118ft (950m), Helvellyn is one of only four peaks in the Lake District that climb above 3000ft (915m). It is a must for any climber or serious walker visiting the area. Striding Edge is one of the most spectacular sights in the Lakes: an arête created by glacial action. Helvellyn's flat summit meant it was chosen by John Leeming and Bert Hinkler in 1926 for the first successful British mountain-top landing and take-off by plane. The photograph looks north-west along Striding Edge with Lower Man at Helvellyn's summit; Thirlmere Water is in the distance. The summit of Helvellyn is marked by a cairn and a cross-shaped shelter visible in the photograph.

FAIRFIELD *above & left*

This massive mountain sits at the head of the valley immediately north of Ambleside. The Fairfield Horseshoe is one of the best-known of the Lake District round-route walks, during which it is possible to see wonderful panoramas across Rydale. The photograph (above) shows the view over the top of the Fairfield Horseshoe into Fairfield Tarn looking west. The photograph (left) shows the Rydal Head cliffs as they drop from a height of over 800 metres. The standard route up takes in the eastern ridge crossing Low Pike, High Pike, Dove Crag and Hart Crag and the return trip down is along the western ridge over Great Rigg, Heron Pike and Nab Scar – from which there are fine views of Rydal and Grasmere.

KIRKSTONE PASS *above*

The photograph above shows the vista due north looking up the Kirkstone Pass towards Brothers Water, the high ground of Patterdale in sight and Ullswater just revealed in the far distance. At 1489ft (454m) it is the highest road pass in the Lakes. Thomas de Quincey wrote about it in *Excursion over Kirkstone Pass in 1807*: "In some parts it is almost frightfully steep; for the road being only the original mountain track of shepherds, gradually widened and improved from age to age… is carried over ground which no engineer, even in alpine countries, would have viewed as practicable." Sited at the top of the pass is the Kirkstone Pass Inn – the third highest pub in England.

SIZERGH CASTLE *right*

Sizergh Castle's south-east facing elevation shows its ornamental pond and gardens. Like so many of Cumbria's castles, Sizergh was originally a pele tower built in the 14th century. It was home to the Strickland family for more than 750 years – passing to them by marriage when an heiress of the Deincourt family married into their ranks bringing the castle first given her family by Henry II in the 1170s. The tower acquired a great hall in 1450, and further additions were made to make the house more habitable in Tudor times. It has a ghost – that of a medieval woman starved to death by her husband. Her screams are still said to echo around the corridors. In addition to the castle there are 14 acres of gardens which were first laid out in the 18th century.

SMALL WATER *above*

Here we see the view north-east from above Harter Fell with the tear-drop shape of Small Water tarn clearly visible. The Vikings settled in Cumbria in the 10th century. The word "tarn" comes from the Norse for tear-drop.

KENTMERE RESERVOIR *right*

In the early 19th century water-power was king in the valley of the Kent: there were 90 mills in the upper course of the river alone. The mills took advantage of the raw power of the river – the Kent drops 1000 feet in 20 miles, and claims to be the fastest-flowing river in the country. But the flow was unpredictable and the Kentmere reservoir was constructed in the mid-19th century to even out the water supply for mill-owners. One of the best-preserved mills can be found further down the valley at Barley Bridge in the centre of Staveley. Today, the Kentmere valley is a quiet backwater and it is difficult to believe that 150 years ago there was a working mill for every 315 people living in the valley.

The photograph shows the reservoir from high above Thornthwaite Beacon. To reach Thornthwaite Beacon the best place to start is in the village of Hartsop. Heading south out of the village the obvious path runs along Pasture Beck, climbing all the time. At the head of this small valley lies Thornthwaite Cove, with steep cliffs blocking the way apart from a route directly up the southernmost slope. At the top the walker reaches Thornthwaite Mouth with the Beacon marking the summit of Thornthwaite Crag a few hundred yards further on.

Northern Lake District

The Northern Lake District provides some of Britain's most awesome glaciated scenery. It includes everything from volcanic mountains to smooth valley floors – lightly populated and a paradise for the walker. Just outside the national park are many historic villages and towns – some of which do not get the attention they deserve because of their proximity to the Lakes. This is a landscape that has had a turbulent history – a fact borne out by the many castles that were once pele towers, designed to provide basic protection to local people when the fierce Border reivers were rampaging.

Penrith *right*

This attractive town, located just outside the Lake District National Park, is a regional centre for the eastern Lakes. Penrith has had a varied and interesting history. Among one of its most famous attractions is the "giant King of all Cumbria" said to be buried in St Andrew's Churchyard. The spot is marked by four stones that are meant to represent wild boar he killed in nearby Inglewood Forest. In the 9th and 10th centuries Penrith was the capital of Cumbria and formed part of the Kingdom of Strathclyde. Raids by Border reivers were common and many of the surrounding mountains had beacons to warn the townsfolk of impending attack.

Penrith Castle was built to defend the town and acted as a sanctuary for the harassed population. At one time it was owned by Richard Duke of Gloucester, later crowned Richard III. The castle is now in ruins. Penrith was the home-town of William Wordsworth's mother and it was here that William and Dorothy Wordsworth and Mary Hutchinson (later to marry William) all attended school.

The "New Streets" area, between Townhead and Scaws, on the side of Beacon Fell, contains many of the town's historic sites. The fellside was used as a burial ground for victims of the plague and many of the street names contain farming references. One of the streets is named Drovers Lane, a reference to Penrith's importance as a market town and its strategic position close to the border with Scotland.

Greystoke *left*

This elegant village a few miles to the west of Penrith has retained a village green with, at its centre, an ancient market cross dating back to late Elizabethan times. Around the green are a number of 17th-century houses, a pub and a school founded in 1838. The village church, dedicated to St Andrew, dates back to the mid-1200s. On Church Road is the Sanctuary Stone – in the past a place where felons could gain sanctuary from pursuers by reaching sanctified ground. A nearby stone is called "Spillers" and is thought to be a plague stone: a place where alms were left to help those in quarantine during an outbreak of the disease.

Greystoke Castle was the seat of the Howard family from the 1500s. The present building was designed by Anthony Salvin. The castle stands in a romantic wooded park and the grounds contain three well-known follies.

BROUGHAM CASTLE *above*

The Roman fort of Brocavum provided stone for the early Brougham Castle when it was built in the 13th century for the Norman Viewpoint family. By 1268 the castle had passed to Robert Clifford, an important figure in the Scottish wars which started in 1296. He carried out a comprehensive programme of building, significantly improving the castle's defences. It survived as a residence until the English Civil War when the building was home to Lady Anne Clifford. Today it is owned by English Heritage.

BASSENTHWAITE *above*

The vista south-west across Bassenthwaite with the heights of Bassenthwaite Common and Skiddaw rising out of the valley pastures and woodland. Bassenthwaite is owned by the National Park Authority and at four miles long (6.5km) and three-quarters of a mile (1.2km) wide is one of the largest lakes in the entire region. The lake is very shallow. There is little settlement around its shores apart from the open-air theatre at Mirehouse – used for a reading in 1974 of *Morte d'Arthur*. Tennyson, who often stayed at Mirehouse, composed much of the poem there. Bassenthwaite is home to the vendace, a rare and endangered species of fish found only here and in Derwent Water. It is also an important site for birds including, during the summer months, England's only breeding ospreys.

BRAITHWAITE *below*

Braithwaite is a village of contrasts with a modern northern district, an older heart and an area of more substantial houses to the south. It is found at the foot of the Whinlatter Pass and enjoys spectacular views of Grisedale Pike and Bassenthwaite. It is an ideal place from which to explore the northern and central Lakes and has plenty of delightful walking routes on its doorstep. It was this part of the Lakes that was particularly beloved of Alfred Wainwright. His remains were scattered on the top of Haystacks – a nearby fell.

SKIDDAW *above*

This view of the massive bulk of Skiddaw looks north-east and includes the northern-most end of Bassenthwaite. Skiddaw is one of the elite group of mountains in England whose summits reach over 3000 feet. It overlooks Keswick and Derwent Water and is a magnet for walkers. In Victorian times ladies used to ascend the mountain by pony.

KESWICK *right*

The bustling town of Keswick is an ideal base for exploring the Lakes. Since 1276 there has been a market in the town of Keswick (from *Cese-wic*, "the cheese town"), and cheese fairs were held regularly until the early 20th century. Medieval Keswick grew up as a ribbon development along either side of the marketplace. By the 19th century small workshops and cottage industries based on wool and leather had developed in the yards adjacent to the houses. The Moot Hall is probably the most imposing of Keswick's buildings. It dates back to 1571 when it was used as a courthouse. Since then it has been used as a market, prison and town hall. William and Dorothy Wordsworth stayed in the town in 1794, Samuel Taylor Coleridge rented part of Greta Hall from 1800-1803, and his brother-in-law, Robert Southey, the Poet Laureate, stayed in Greta Hall for 40 years. While living there that he wrote the famous children's story, *The Three Bears*.

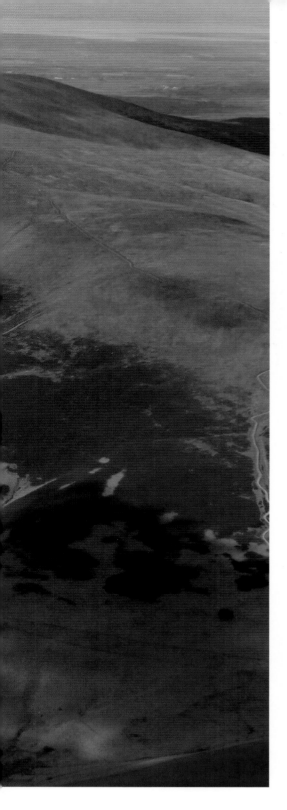

ULLSWATER *right*

Ullswater is the second largest lake in the Lake District. It is serpentine, making three distinct turns, and is 7.5 miles (12km) long; about three-quarters of a mile (1.2km) wide on average and reaches its greatest depth of 205ft (62m) at Howtown. The name Ullswater is said to derive from "Ulf's water" in memory of Ulf – a Nordic chief who ruled the area. This is yet another proof of the Lake District's deep Viking roots. Even the area's hardy Herdwick sheep (grey wool with white faces) are said to have been introduced by Scandinavian settlers. Before the Vikings, the Romans had a strong presence here. As well as the settlements that line the lake the area also boasts the world's second largest leadmine in Glenridding (which means "valley of the bracken").

Many of the Lake District's most famous fell walks start near Ullswater, including the magnificent trek up to Helvellyn's summit via Striding Edge. There are also many less strenuous paths around the lake, rich in spectacle, peace and wildlife.

The daffodils growing along the Glencoyne shore of Ullswater inspired Wordsworth to write *I wandered lonely as a cloud*, one of the best-known poems in the English language.

It was on Ullswater that Donald Campbell broke the 200mph world water speed record in 1955. Far less adventurous sports are the order of the day now and the lake is much used for sailing, sailboarding, fishing and cruising.

POOLEY BRIDGE *left*

The village of Pooley Bridge, viewed here from over Ullswater looking north-east, straddles the river Eamont at the northern end of Ullswater as it flows on to Penrith. The name Pooley Bridge derives from a large pool that used to be found at the mouth of the river Eamont just before it flows out of Ullswater. The bridge dates from the 16th century. Once the village derived its income from fishing and farming and there is still a thriving business serving the needs of anglers who fish for the trout, salmon and the much rarer schelly (a kind of freshwater herring) that live in these waters.

The village consists of two main streets lined with delightful old stone houses. One hundred years ago the Ullswater Navigation and Transit Company steamers provided transport for mail, goods and people around Ullswater. Today these same steamers have been converted to carry passengers between Pooley Bridge, Howtown and Glenridding. The village's famous boathouse attracts visitors and photographers from all over the world.

MOSEDALE VIADUCT *right*

Mosedale origin's are Norse and date from 900. Its name comes from the Norse word, *nosi*, for peat moss. Most of the valley to the east of Mosedale contains peat bogs – the remains of a former lake that dried up thousands of years ago. Tiny Mosedale village boasts an early 18th-century Quaker meeting house with fine Tuscan sandstone columns. Nearby, on the summit of volcanic Carrock Fell, are the remains of an oval-shaped Celtic hillfort, the largest in Cumbria. A narrow road leads from the hamlet of Mosedale, follows the river Caldew up the Mosedale valley, and ends at the former Carrock tungsten mine. Lead, copper and small amounts of gold were mined here. The 12-arch Mosedale viaduct is the largest structure along the old Kendal-Penrith railway line. There is an energetic campaign to re-open the link with estimates of between 250,000 and 450,000 passengers a year as potential users of the railway

CASTLERIGG STONE CIRCLE *above*

Castlerigg Stone Circle is one of the most powerful and spectacular prehistoric monuments in Britain, and is the most visited stone circle in Cumbria. The stone circle is on the level top of a low hill with views across to Skiddaw, Blencathra and Lonscale Fell. There are 38 stones in a circle approximately 100ft (30m) in diameter. Within the ring is a rectangle of a further 10 standing stones. The tallest stone is 7.5ft (2.3m) high. It was probably built around 3000BC – the beginning of the later Neolithic Period – and is one of the earliest stone circles in Britain. It is important in terms of megalithic astronomy and geometry, as the construction contains significant astronomical alignments. Castlerigg Stone Circle was bought in 1913 by a consortium including Canon Hardwick Rawnsley, co-founder of the National Trust.

SHARP EDGE *right*

One of the Lake District's best ridges is Sharp Edge on the eastern side of Blencathra. Experienced walkers advise a clockwise circuit of the ridge. Sharp Edge is often described as one of the most challenging walks in the Lakes – not because of steep slopes or boggy ground (both of which can be found) but because of its situation. This poses a real danger to those who attempt it wearing inadequate gear – a problem in the summer when the area's population swells with tourists.

First published in 2007 by Myriad Books Limited, 35 Bishopsthorpe Road, London SE26 4PA

Photographs copyright © Simon Kirwan
Text copyright © Jerome Monahan

Jerome Monahan has asserted his right under the Copyright, Designs and Patents Act 1998 to be identified as the author of this work.

ISBN 1 84746 017 8

EAN 978 1 84746 017 2

Designed by Jerry Goldie Graphic Design

Printed in China

www.myriadbooks.com